Body Talk

In Your Genes

GENETICS AND REPRODUCTION

Steve Parker

Chicago, Illinois

Published by Raintree,
a division of Capstone Global Library, LLC.
Chicago, Illinois

For information, address the publisher
Raintree, 100 N. LaSalle, Suite 1200
Chicago, IL 60602
Customer Service 888–363–4266
Visit our website at www.raintreelibrary.com

Printed and bound in the United States of America
in North Mankato, Minnesota. 092012 006924

14 13 12
10 9 8 7 6 5 4 3 2 1

Library of Congress Cataloging-in-Publication Data
Parker, Steve.
In your genes! : genetics and reproduction / Steve Parker.
p. cm. — (Body talk)
Includes index.
ISBN 1-4109-1876-9 (lib. bdg.)
ISBN 978-1-4109-1876-5 (lib. bdg.)
ISBN 1-4109-1883-1 (pbk.)
ISBN 978-1-4109-1883-3 (pbk.)

1. Human genetics—Juvenile literature. 2. Human reproduction—Juvenile literature. I. Title. II. Series: Parker, Steve. Body talk.
QH431.P35 2006
611'.01816—dc22

2005027517

Acknowledgments
The publishers would like to thank the following for permission to reproduce photographs:
Alamy Images pp.18; 5, 4-5 (Visions of America); Corbis pp. 6-7, 8; 21 (Luis Enrique Ascui/ Reuters), pp. 26-27 (Walter Smith), p. 36 (Bettmann), p. 42 (Gabe Palmer), pp. 14-15 (Charles O'Rear); Getty Images pp. 5, 15, 17, 24, 26 (Photodisc), p. 31 (Photonica), pp. 32-33 (Taxi), p. 41 (Stone), pp. 42-43 (The Image Bank); Getty Images News pp. 16-17; Science Photo Library pp. 14, 22; 5, 23 (TEK Image), p. 6 (David Scharf), p. 7 (Simon Fraser), pp. 9, 20, 28, 29 (Steve Gschmeissner), p. 9 (Andrew Syred), pp. 10-11, 34 (Eye of Science), p. 13, (Corbis/Digital Art), p. 12, (A. Barrington Brown), p. 16 (Andrew Syred), p. 21 (Dr Paul Andrews, University of Dundee), p. 25 (Du Cane Medical Imaging LTD), p. 35 (Zephyr), pp. 37, 38 (Edelmann), p. 39 (Garry Watson), p. 40 (Dr Najeeb Layyous), p. 39 (Alex Bartel); The Advertising Archives, p. 24.
Cover photograph of baby reproduced with permission of Masterfile/Pierre Tremblay.
Artwork by Darren Lingard and Jeff Edwards.

The paper used to print this book comes from sustainable resources.

Disclaimer
All the Internet addresses (URLs) given in this book were valid at the time of going to press. However, due to the dynamic nature of the Internet, some addresses may have changed, or sites may have ceased to exist since publication. While the author and publishers regret any inconvenience this may cause readers, no responsibility for any such changes can be accepted by either the author or the publishers.

Dedicated to the memory of Lucy Owen

Contents

Nobody Like Me 4

Instructions for Life 6

Pairs of Genes 16

Passing on Genes 26

New Baby 36

Find Out More 44

Glossary 45

Index 48

Any words appearing in the text in bold, **like this,** are explained in the glossary. You can also look out for them in "Body language" at the bottom of each page.

Nobody Like Me

Have you looked in the mirror today? Looking back at you would be a very familiar and unique face. Even if you searched all over the world, there would be no one else with your looks and physical appearance.

There are plenty of human bodies to check out, more than six billion worldwide. (If you said "Hi" to each one nonstop, it would take you 200 years!) But they are all different. Even the people who are most similar to each other, identical twins, are not exactly the same.

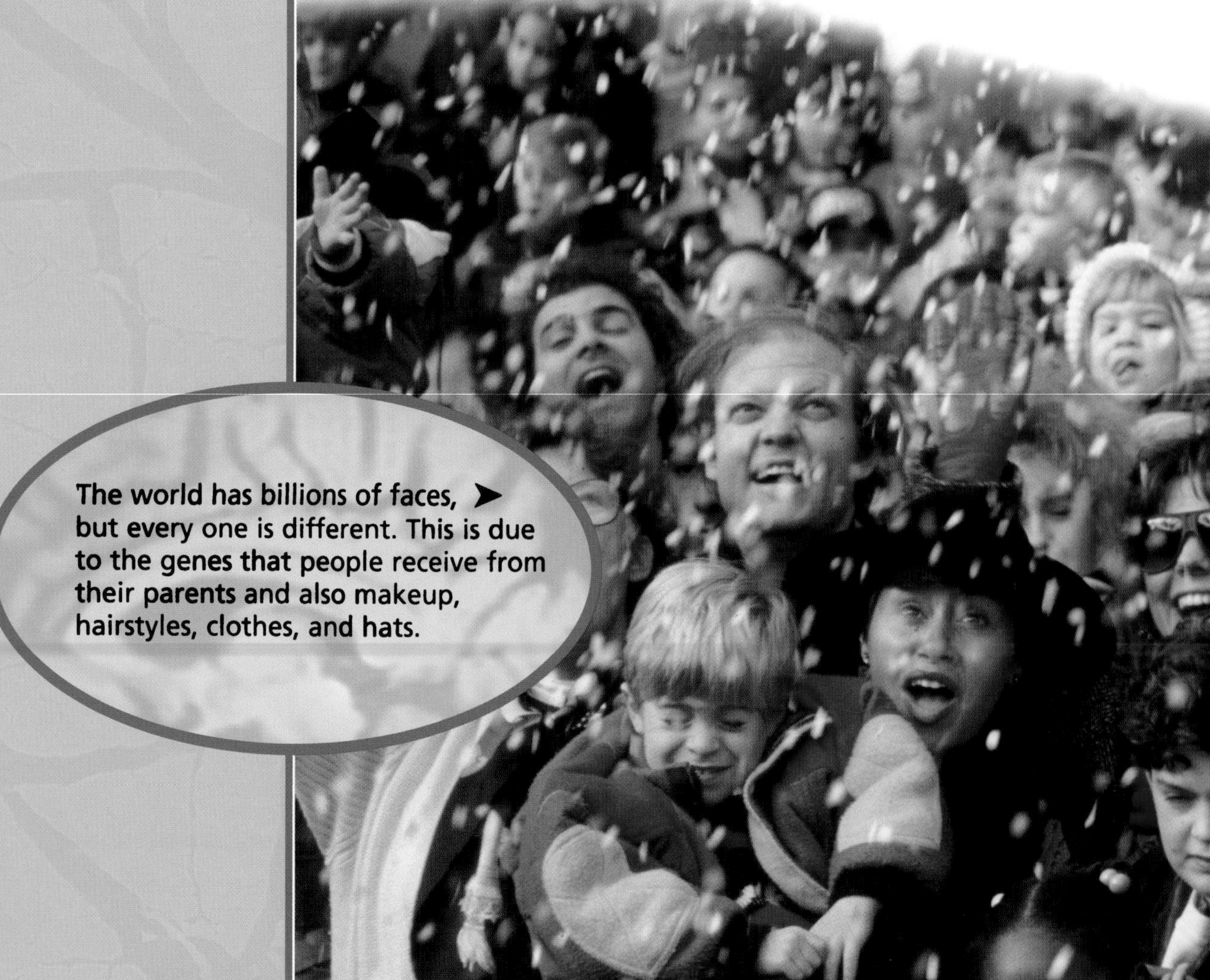

The world has billions of faces, ➤ but every one is different. This is due to the genes that people receive from their parents and also makeup, hairstyles, clothes, and hats.

genes instructions for how the body grows, develops, and works. Smallest unit that can pass characteristics from one person to another.

Basically similar

We are all unique, yet we are all similar too. Human bodies have two eyes, a nose, a mouth, arms, legs, fingernails, and toenails. This basic body design for people is the same everywhere. So people are different yet similar. In particular, you are more like members of your family than people you are not related to.

Deep inside

The main reason for groups of people being basically similar, but different as individuals, is deep inside us in our **genes.** When we understand what genes are and how they work, we can begin to understand what makes each of us an individual.

Find out later

What needs 47 pairs, while you only have 23?

What is a genetic fingerprint?

Why do some people have dimples?

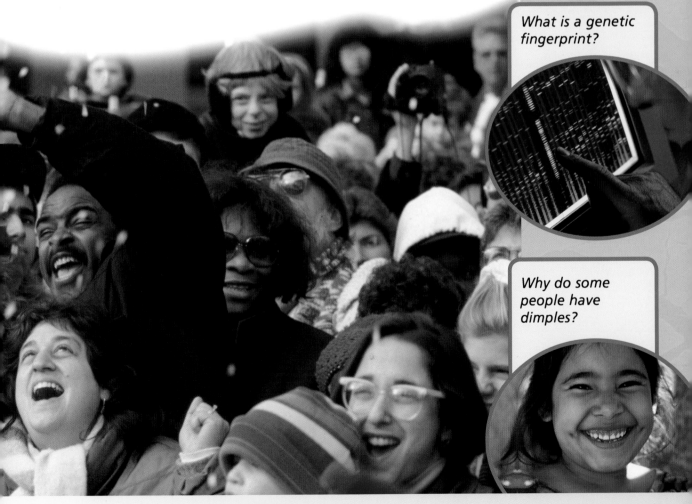

Instructions for Life

How many genes?

The human body has about 30,000 genes. All together, they form the **human genome**, the complete set of instructions for how the body grows and lives. All other living things have genes, too. Many have more genes than we do, even if they are smaller than we are.

Rice plant	over 40,000
Human	about 30,000
Mouse	about 29,000
Nematode (tiny worm)	19,100
Fruit fly (below)	13,600

Imagine you are building a robot or computer. In front of you is a large table covered with pieces of wire, microchips, circuit boards, screws, and other items. These are pieces of hardware, the physical things for building what you need.

To put them together, you'll need a set of instructions in the form of a building plan. Once the computer is assembled, it needs to be programmed with a set of working instructions. These tell it how to carry out tasks like word processing, graphics, and games.

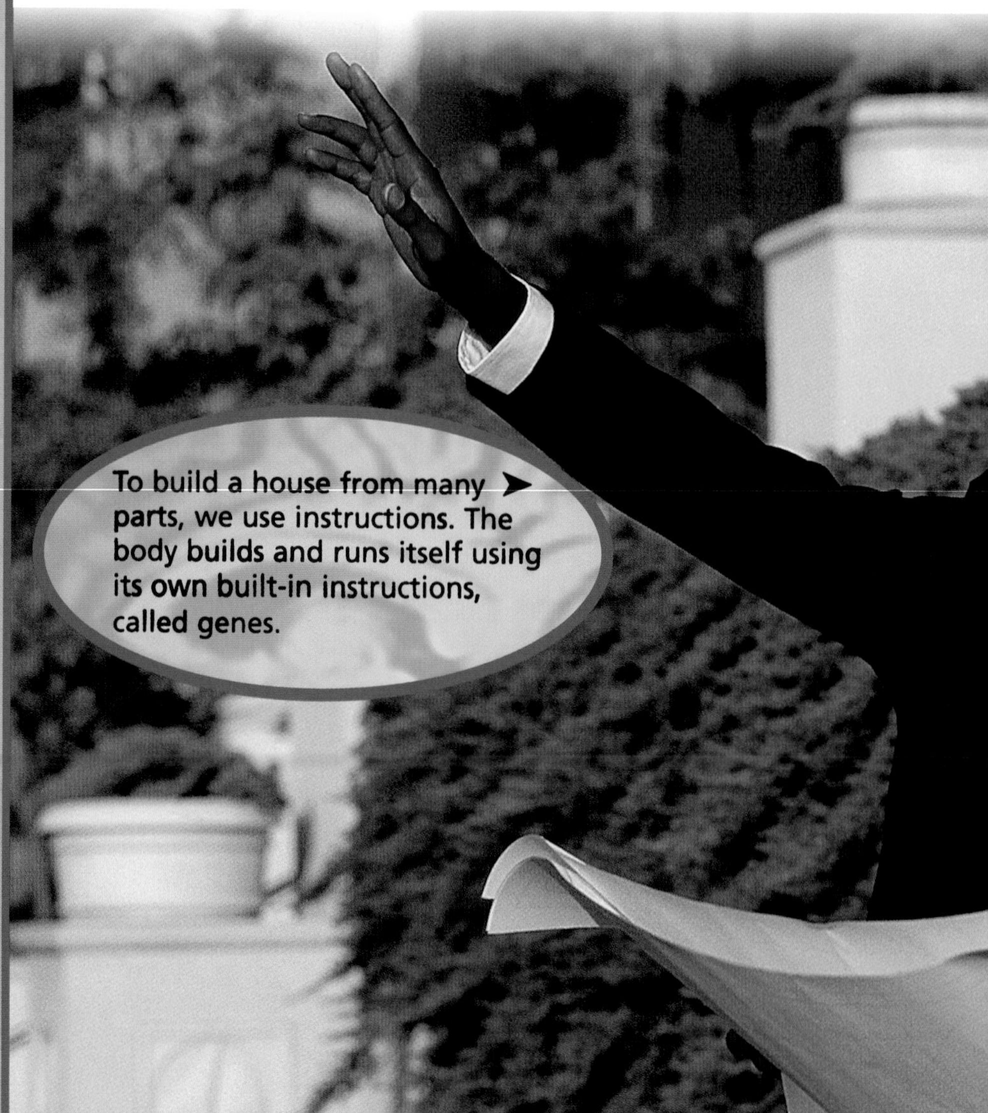

To build a house from many parts, we use instructions. The body builds and runs itself using its own built-in instructions, called genes.

DNA deoxyribonucleic acid. Molecule that contains the genes.

Building and running

The body needs plans and instructions, too. Its building plans show it how to grow and develop from a baby to a child to an adult. Its working instructions tell it how to work and run itself day by day, as it carries out essential tasks like breathing, eating, and moving. The instructions for a machine are usually on sheets of paper or a screen. Your body's instructions are inside you, and are called its **genes.** They are in the form of a chemical substance known as **DNA.**

Different types of genes

Genes don't only affect the body's outer appearance of skin color and adult height. They also carry instructions for how the inner parts of the body are made, such as the stomach, lungs, heart, liver, kidneys, and hundreds more.

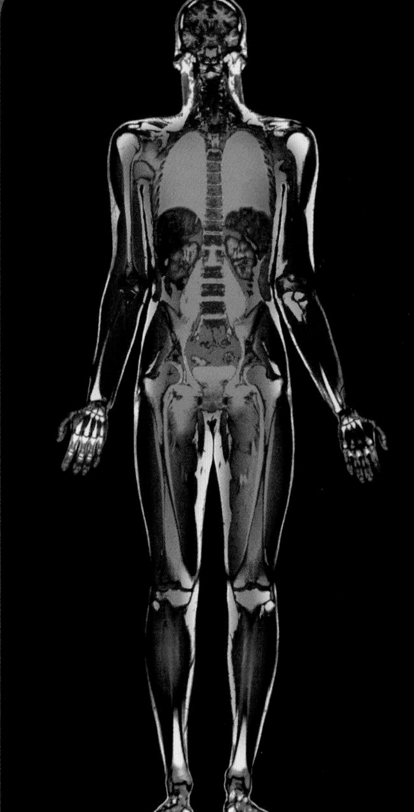

Genes on or off?

Any big machine has lots of small parts working together inside. A jumbo jet has over four million. But your human body beats this easily. It has over 50 trillion, perhaps as many as 75 trillion. To fit them all in, each working part is microscopic. About 30 of them placed end to end would stretch across the dot on this i. These tiny parts are called **cells.**

Different cells

Your body has many different kinds of cells inside. These have different shapes, sizes and jobs. Thousands of long, thin muscle cells make up your muscles. Even longer, thinner **nerve** cells form your nerves. Spider-shaped bone cells make your bones, and so on. There are over different 200 kinds of cells that form all your body parts.

Building up features

Millions of tiny skin cells form patterns of swirly ridges on our fingers, called fingerprints (below). These are controlled mostly by genes. Everyone has different fingerprints, which are often used for security identification.

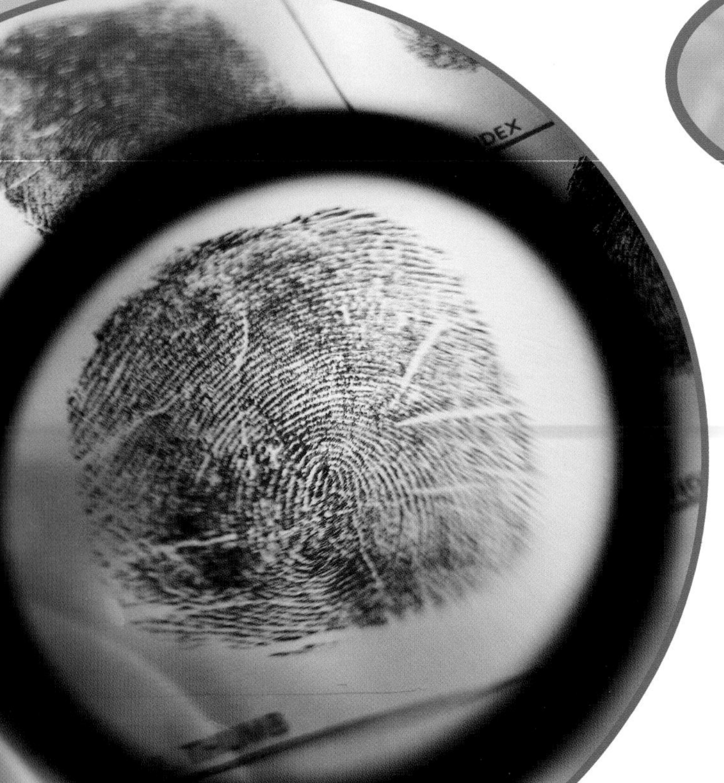

Certain cells switch on only ➤ the genes that they need to build the part of the body they are in charge of, such as skin or hair.

Body language

nerves stringlike tissues that carry messages around the body as tiny pulses of electricity

Take what you need

Each of these tiny cells has all 30,000 of the body's **genes** inside in the form of the chemical **DNA.** But each cell does not use them all. It uses only the ones that tell it how to do its own specialized job. In a muscle cell, the muscle genes are switched on, but the rest are switched off. Likewise, a skin cell has the skin genes turned on, but the others do not work. This gene-switching happens all over the body, in millions of different cells.

Life and death

Your genes tell each cell how to grow, what shape to become, what job to do, and when to die. **Red blood cells** (above) carry life-giving **oxygen** from your lungs to all your body parts. They all live for about the same time, three months, then they die as they are replaced by more red cells. This life span information is programmed into all body cells.

oxygen gas that makes up one-fifth of air, and which the body needs
red blood cells cells specialized to carry oxygen around the body

Size of DNA

- DNA is incredibly thin, but amazingly long.
- If half a million strands of DNA were put side by side they would measure only 0.04 in (1 mm) across.
- If all the 46 strands of DNA in one single cell were joined end to end, they would stretch about 6.6 ft (2 m).
- If the same was done to all the DNA in all the cells of the whole body, then the DNA would stretch from the Earth to the Sun and back more than 100 times!

Where are genes?

You might be used to following instructions which are words and pictures. Of course the **gene's** instructions are not words or pictures. They are in the form of the threadlike chemical substance called **DNA.**

There are 46 different strands of DNA inside each cell. These strands are called **chromosomes**. Each chromosome has its own set of **genes**, and between all 46, they contain 30,000 genes.

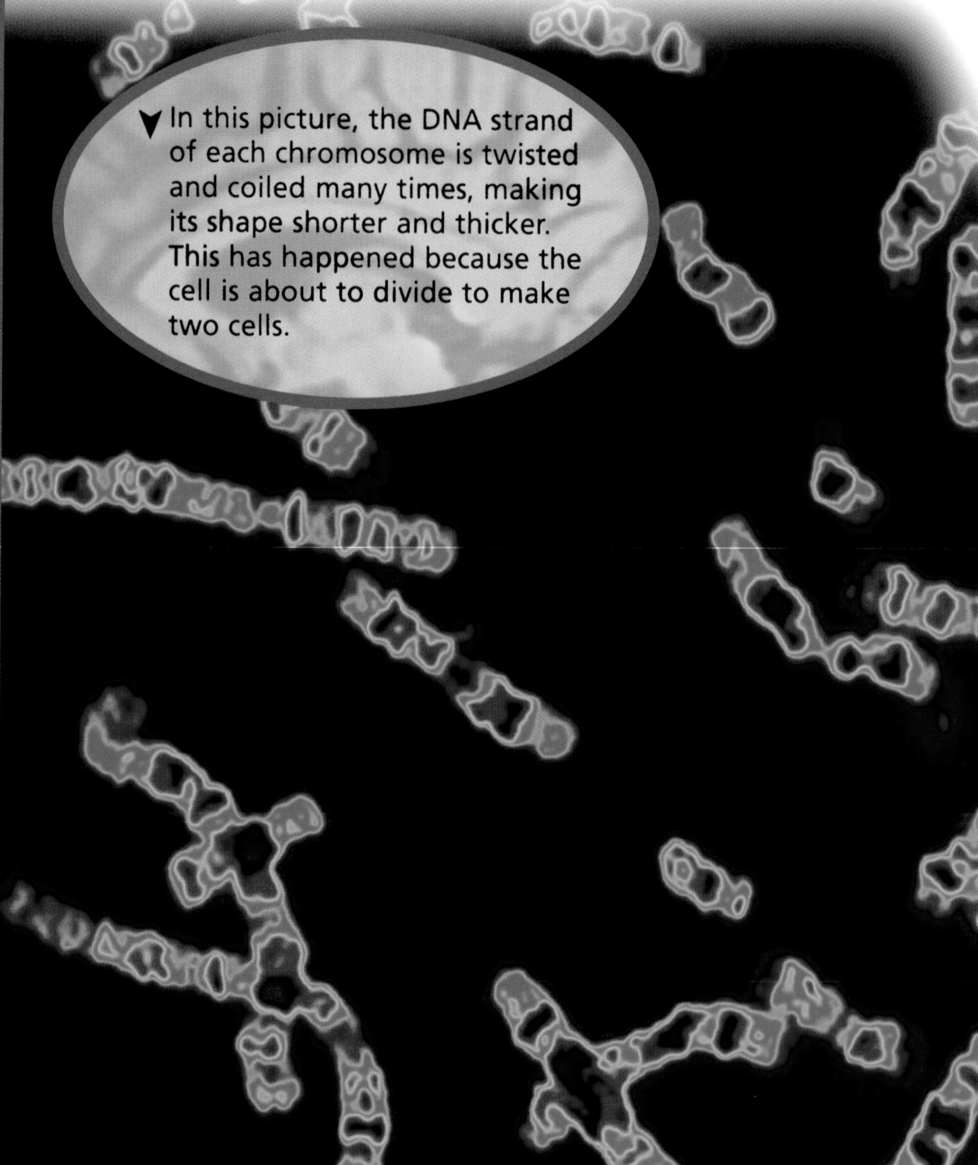

▼ In this picture, the DNA strand of each chromosome is twisted and coiled many times, making its shape shorter and thicker. This has happened because the cell is about to divide to make two cells.

chromosome thread of DNA that contains thousands of genes

Changing shape

Chromosomes can change shape. Usually their DNA is unraveled long and thin, like pieces of stretched-out string. These are very difficult to see under the microscope. But if the cell is about to divide, as shown later, the chromosomes change. In each one the DNA strand twists into a thicker, shorter coil, like twisting an elastic band tight.

In the control center

The 46 chromosomes do not float about anywhere in the **cell.** They are inside the **nucleus.** The nucleus is usually a rounded blob somewhere near the middle of the cell. It contains the chromosomes, which have the genes that tell all parts of the cell what to do.

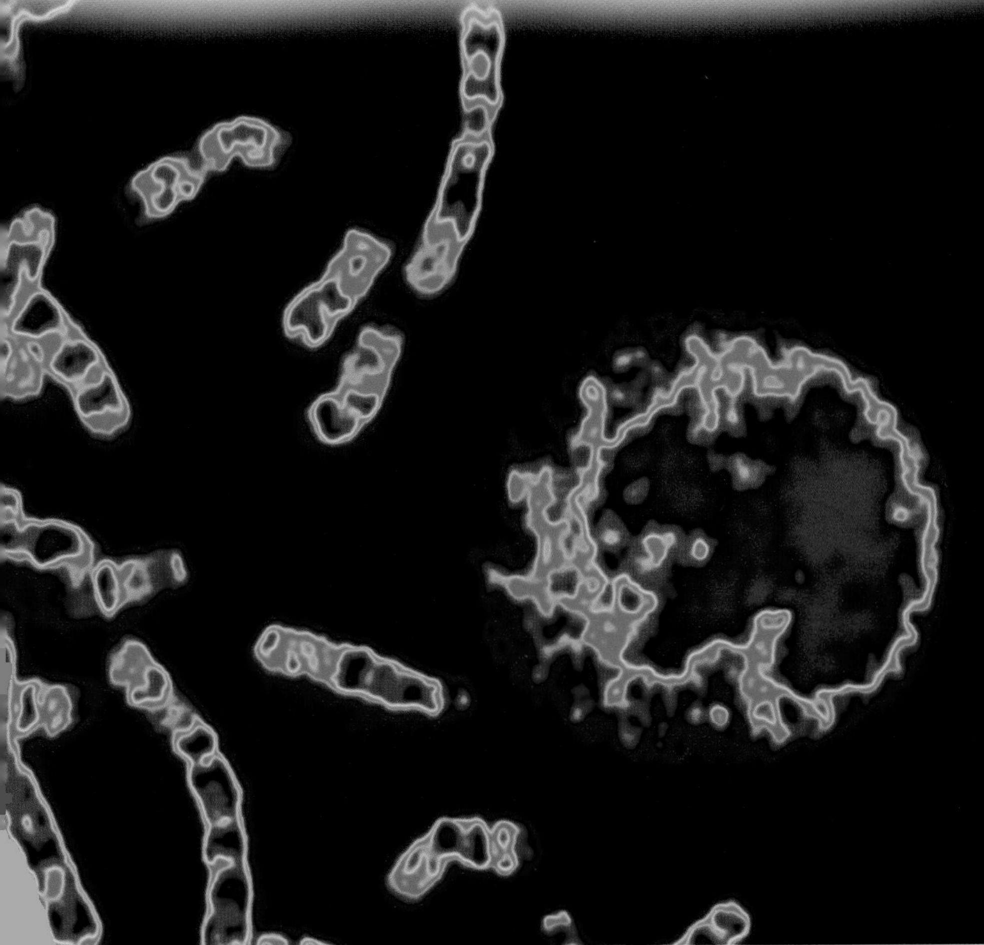

Different lengths

The chromosomes (strands of DNA) inside each cell are not all the same length. Chromosome number 1 is the longest DNA strand, with 245 million pairs of **bases.** Number 2 is slightly shorter, and so on. The average stretched-out length for one chromosome is almost 2 in (47 mm).

nucleus control center of a cell. It contains the DNA.
bases four chemicals that form the rungs of the ladder in DNA. Each rung is made of two bases.

What are genes?

If 1 = A, 2 = B, 3 = C, and so on, what does 7 5 14 5 spell? This is information or instructions written in code. Codes can be in many different forms, such as numbers, letters, words, diagrams, and even chemicals. **DNA** contains its **genetic** information in the form of a chemical code.

Junk DNA

In each cell, there is far more DNA than is needed for the body's 30,000 genes. It is like a book with many more blank pages than written ones. However, the blank pages, called junk DNA, may have useful jobs controlling and organizing the genes.

Twisted ladder

Each long strand of DNA in a chromosome is shaped like a ladder which has been twisted like a corkscrew. This shape is called a **double helix.** The two long sides of the ladder are the same throughout. But the cross-parts or rungs of the ladder are not. They are made of small chemical units called **bases,** joined together in pairs. There are four kinds of bases. They are known by the first letters of their chemical names: A (**adenine**), T (**thymine**), C (**cytosine**), and G (**guanine**).

SECRET OF LIFE!

In 1953, two scientists, James Watson (left) and Francis Crick (right), worked out the mysterious, ladderlike shape of DNA. In the year 2000 Watson and Crick's work was voted one of the top three scientific discoveries of the 20th century.

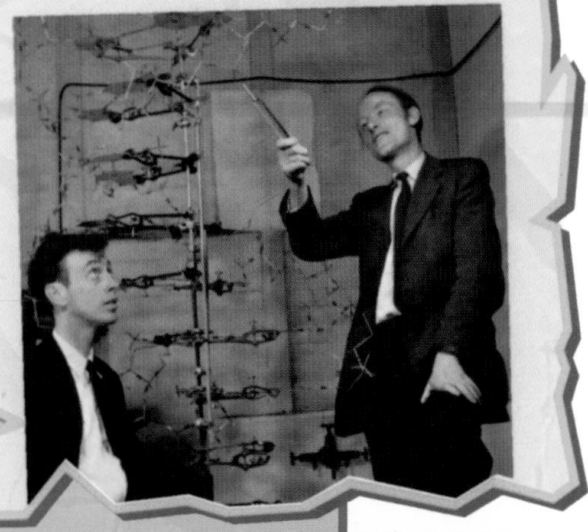

Genetic code

A **gene** is one small section of a strand of DNA. The order of the bases along this small section provides important information. If we write them out as letters, GACTTAGGCTAC for example, they look pretty strange. An average gene is 3,000 bases long. That's a lot of As, Cs, Ts and Gs. It would be a very long word that looks like nonsense to us. But to the **cell**, the order of the 3,000 bases is a single gene or genetic instruction, that tells the cell how to do something.

This is how your cells know things such as what shape your features should be and what color your hair will be. It is all written in your genetic code.

genetic to do with genes

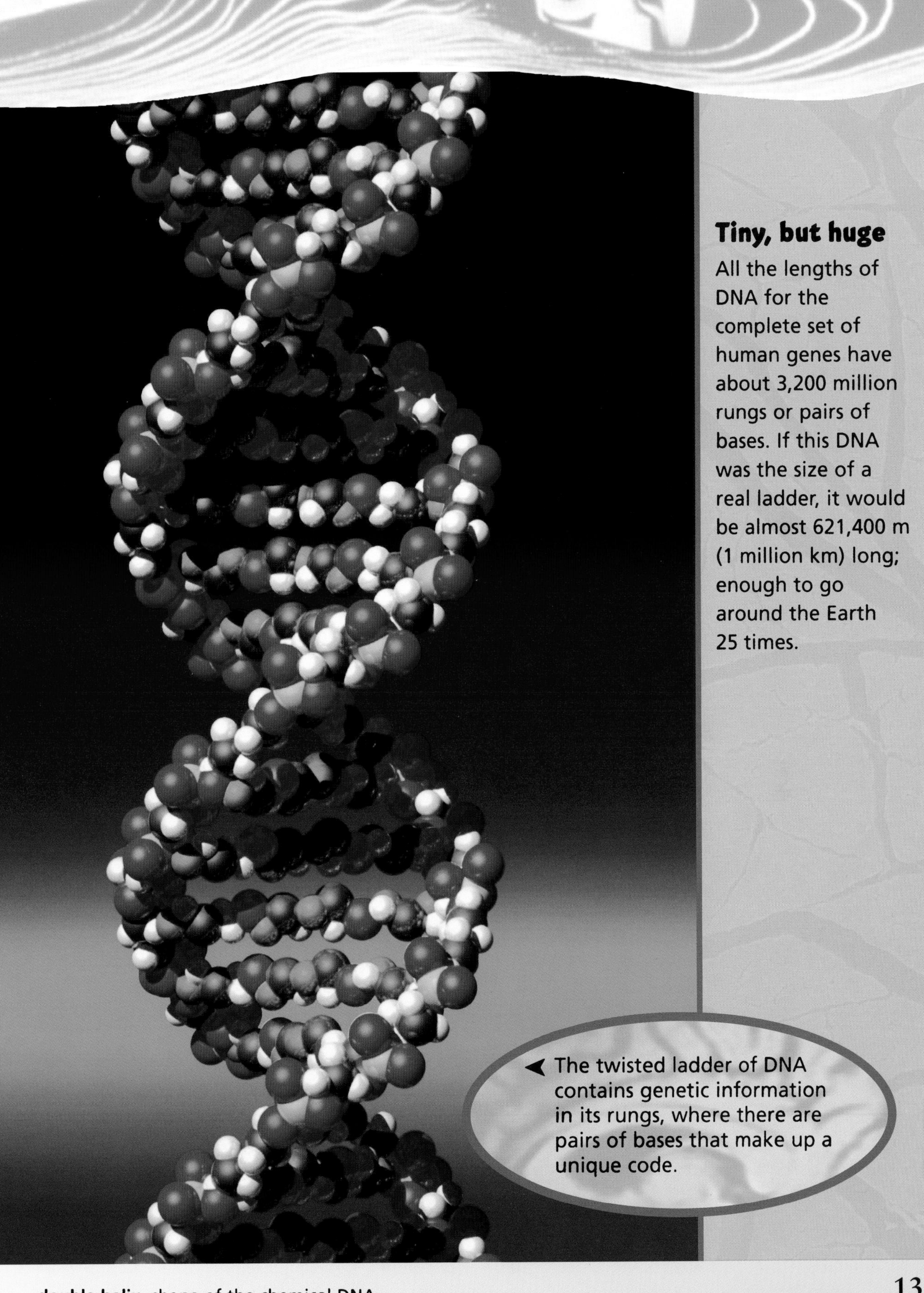

Tiny, but huge

All the lengths of DNA for the complete set of human genes have about 3,200 million rungs or pairs of bases. If this DNA was the size of a real ladder, it would be almost 621,400 m (1 million km) long; enough to go around the Earth 25 times.

The twisted ladder of DNA contains genetic information in its rungs, where there are pairs of bases that make up a unique code.

double helix shape of the chemical DNA

How genes work

The plans for a house would be of little use on their own, with no one to use them. You need to make copies of the plans and give them out to people with the skills to build each part. These people then read the plans, make the different parts shown, and fit them together to make the finished result. **Genetic** information is similar. It is also copied, read, and used to make its finished results.

Reading genes

One **gene** is one part of the string of **DNA** in a **chromosome.** The DNA is a model, or template, for the building of a similar substance, **RNA.** These RNA molecules are sent out of the **nucleus** to other parts of the cell.

Making new parts

Inside a cell, such as the plasma cell below, tiny blob-shaped ribosomes are like assembly lines in factories. They use information in the genes to build new proteins. The proteins are then joined together.

nucleus

ribosomes

A body cell uses its genetic instructions to build up new substances, in the way that factory production lines assemble cars and other products.

RNA ribonucleic acid. It uses DNA instructions to build proteins inside cells.

Building work

In the cell, the RNA attaches to ball-shaped parts called **ribosomes**. The ribosomes use the instructions from the RNA to join together very small, simple chemical substances in the cell, to build a bigger, more complicated result. The finished result is a **protein,** one of the building block substances for the body.

Just as bricklayers or carpenters have different tasks when building a house, different genes have their own instructions for making different kinds of proteins. These various proteins make up your different body parts, such as muscles, nerves, skin, and bones.

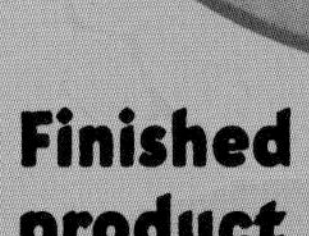

Finished product

Several genes control the color of your eyes. They contain the instructions for making the colored substances, called **pigments,** at the front of the eye. These special genes are only switched on in the cells of the colored part of the eye, the iris.

ribosomes parts within a cell, where simple chemicals are joined together to make proteins according to RNA instructions

Pairs of Genes

Each of your body's **cells** contains two full sets of genetic instructions, as strands of **DNA** called **chromosomes.** Apart from a couple of special cells (which we will look at later), every cell has two complete sets of chromosomes, with two complete sets of genes.

From the parents

The two complete sets of chromosomes in a cell make a pair. One set of 23 chromosones matches the other set of 23, to make 46 chromosomes in every cell.

The reason for having two sets goes back to when a human body begins its life as a single microscopic cell called the **fertilized egg.**

In pairs

The chromosomes from a single human cell are usually spread around the **nucleus.** When pictures of them are taken through a microscope, the chromosomes can be matched up into pairs, because each member of a pair looks like the other.

On a sports team, each player has an opponent in the other team doing the same job. Likewise in a human body cell, there are two sets of genes, each with much the same task.

Body language **fertilized egg** egg cell joined with a sperm cell

In the egg, one of the sets of 23 chromosomes came from the mother. The other set of 23 came from the father.

Two genes for one

Because you have a pair of chromosomes in each cell, each gene is in a pair, too. For many genes, both members of the pair are exactly the same. They contain the same information for making the same part of the body, such as your eye color. But in some cases the members of the pair are slightly different. This is partly what makes you unique.

More and less

Other animals, and plants, too, have pairs of chromosomes like us. But most do not have 23 pairs. The number of pairs is not linked to the size of the animal or plant, or to its total number of genes.

Fruit fly	4 pairs
Housefly	6 pairs
Cat	19 pairs
Human	23 pairs
Horse	32 pairs
Dog	39 pairs
Pigeon	40 pairs
Goldfish	47 pairs
Crayfish	100 pairs

Dimple test

When you smile, do you have dimples in your cheeks? This depends on your genes. If both alleles of the dimple gene are dimple, you will have them. Even if you only have one dimple gene, you will still get them, because the dimple allele is more dominant than the no-dimple one.

Taking over

Do your earlobes hang low and wobble to and fro? It depends on your **genes.** You have a double set of genes in every body cell. So you have two genes giving instructions for every feature, such as whether you have dangly earlobes or not. But these genes might not be giving exactly the same instructions.

Some genes have several different versions, known as **alleles.** You received one allele from your mother and the other from your father. Your earlobe (or other feature) shape depends on how these alleles work together. They both have the instructions to make the same part, but one may want it to be large and the other may want it to be small.

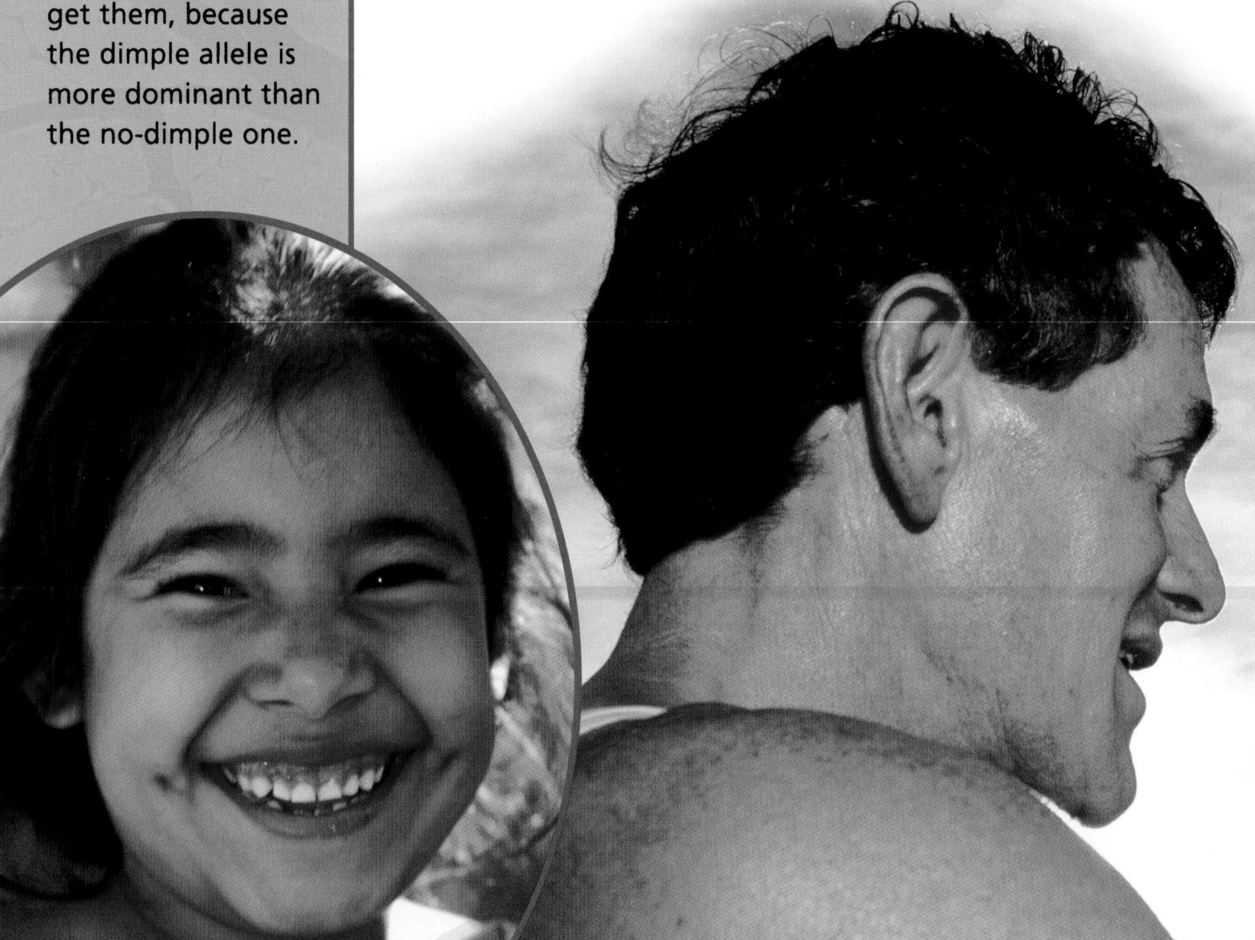

allele version of a gene that controls how a certain body part is made or works

Trial of strength

If both genes for earlobes are the dangly alleles, you will have dangly earlobes. If both genes are small, your earlobes will be small. But what if there is one allele for dangly and the other is for small?

The small earlobe allele is stronger or **dominant,** compared to the dangly one, which is weaker or **recessive.** So the dominant one will win, and you will have small earlobes. Many genes act in a dominant or recessive way. It makes genetics quite complicated.

Which gene is boss?

In this table, you can see that the dominant version of a gene overpowers the recessive one. The recessive result only happens if someone has two recessive versions of the gene.

GENE FOR	DOMINANT ALLELE (stronger version)	RECESSIVE ALLELE (weaker version)
Hair color	Darker hair	Lighter hair
Hair loss (men)	Early hair loss	Late hair loss
Eyelash length	Longer eyelashes	Shorter eyelashes
Arch of foot	Up-curved arch	Flatter arch

The older man has recessive dangly earlobe alleles from both sets of genes, and so has long, dangly lobes.

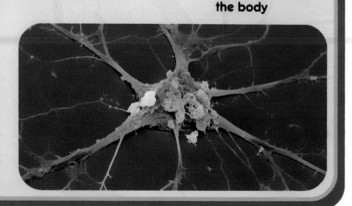

New cells for old

Every second, five million tiny parts of you die. They are microscopic cells that have done their jobs and their lives have come to an end. But every second, about the same number of new cells are made to take their place.

The body constantly maintains, repairs, and renews itself, by replacing old cells with new ones. It does this using various types of **stem cells.** These are cells which are specialized to make more cells, by dividing in half, and then growing back to full size. The process is called **cell division.**

How long do cells live?

Different kinds of cells in the body live for different amounts of time before they are replaced by cell division. This time span is built into the genes.

TYPE OF CELL	LIFE SPAN
Cheek inner lining cell	12 hours
Stomach inner lining cell	2 days
Germ-eating white blood cell	12 days
Taste cell on tongue	30 days
Outer skin cell (epidermis)	30 days
Red blood cell	120 days
Liver cell	18 months
Bone cell	10 years
Nerve cell (below)	Same lifetime as the body

Divide and multiply

As a stem cell divides, it copies all the tiny parts inside it, including the **nucleus** and all the **DNA,** into both the new cells. Each of the two new cells then has a choice. It can stay as a stem cell, and divide again. Or it can start to become specialized, by switching on certain genes which make it into a nerve cell, muscle cell, bone cell or another type of cell. The choice depends on what your body needs at that time.

This cell is just dividing ➤ into two. Each new nucleus has the same DNA, but the two cells may end up switching on different genes to do different tasks.

cell division one cell splits to make two cells

Stem cells

Stem cells have the ability to become almost any kind of specialized cell. This does not work the other way round. Cells that are already specialized, like muscle, bone, and blood cells, cannot become stem cells. Medical scientists (below) are studying how to train stem cells to make the specialized cells that ill people need to rebuild damaged parts.

stem cells cells that can make specialized cells, such as blood or skin cells

Copy, copy, copy

When you get a new cell phone, you need a set of instructions. **Cells** in the body are the same. Each one needs its own instructions, or **genes.** When a cell divides, as shown on the previous page, part of this division requires that the genes, in other words, the **DNA,** be copied.

DNA unzipped

DNA is designed to copy itself. This is possible because of the pairs of **bases** that form the rungs of the DNA ladder. On each rung, the base T always links to A, and C always links to G.

To copy itself, the strand of DNA first unzips by breaking the link between each pair of bases. This produces two half-ladders. Then the half-ladders each build a new half, to become a **double helix** again.

Two sets

Before a cell divides, its 23 pairs of DNA strands, the chromosomes, copy themselves. Then the strands coil up thicker and shorter and each moves next to its partner. As splitting happens, one single set of chromosomes moves into each resulting cell. This process is called **mitosis.**

To copy itself, DNA splits ➤ down the middle. Each existing half builds up a new half that is an exact copy of the one it used to be attached to.

Body language **DNA polymerase** enzyme that enables DNA to copy itself

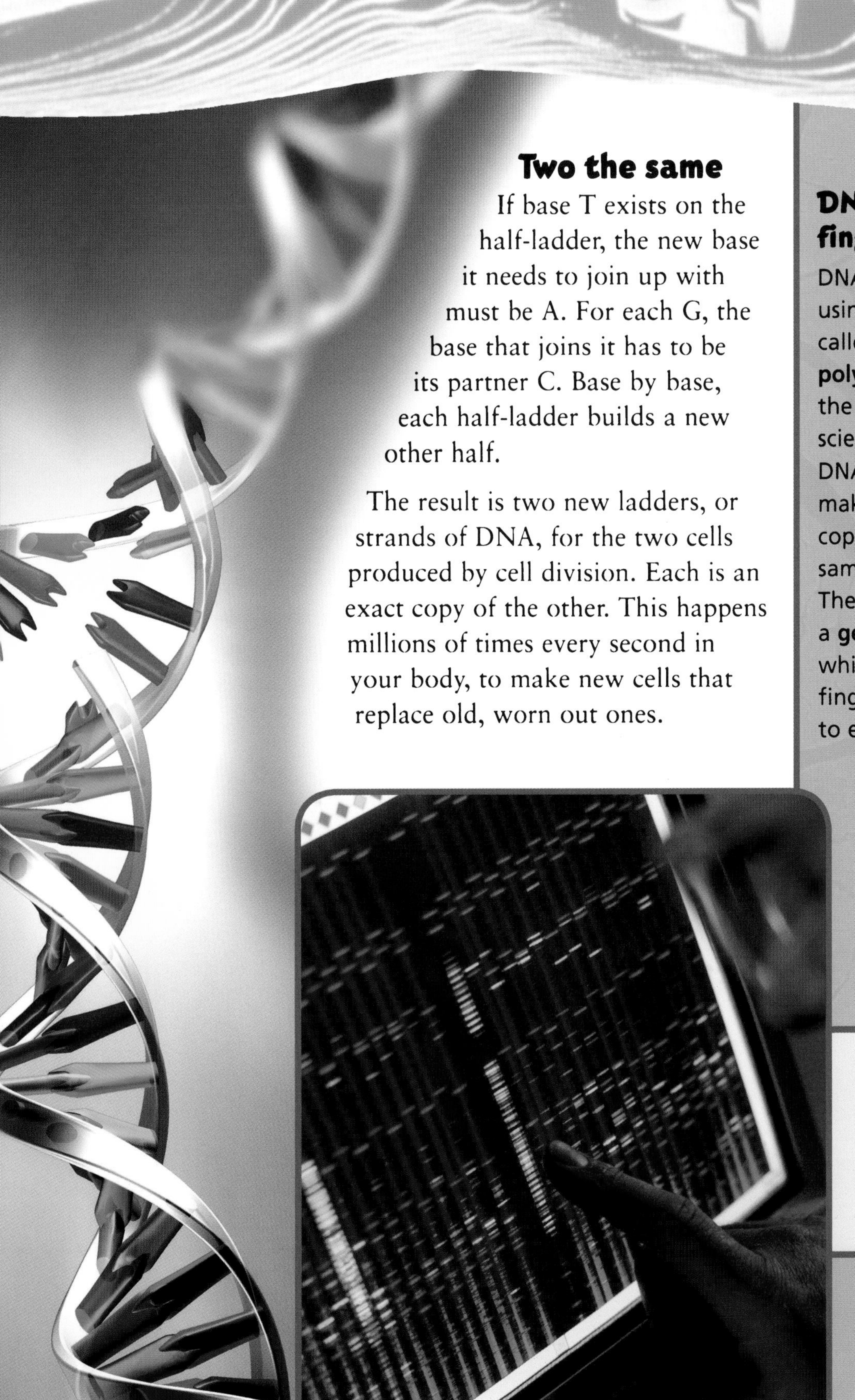

Two the same

If base T exists on the half-ladder, the new base it needs to join up with must be A. For each G, the base that joins it has to be its partner C. Base by base, each half-ladder builds a new other half.

The result is two new ladders, or strands of DNA, for the two cells produced by cell division. Each is an exact copy of the other. This happens millions of times every second in your body, to make new cells that replace old, worn out ones.

DNA fingerprints

DNA copies itself using a substance called **DNA polymerase.** In the laboratory, scientists can use DNA polymerase to make millions of copies of a tiny sample of DNA. They can then make a **genetic fingerprint,** which like a real fingerprint, is unique to each person.

Genetic fingerprints show up like the bar code of a product in the supermarket.

genetic fingerprint code on a strand of DNA, unique to each person

Not exact copies

If you copy hundreds of words, sooner or later you will probably make a mistake. You might miss a letter, or swap two words, or even leave out a whole sentence. **DNA** is similar. Usually its copying process, called **DNA replication,** is exact. But sometimes there is a mistake.

Kinds of errors

There are several kinds of copying mistakes that happen in DNA. One of the chemical units called **bases** might get broken off, or not attach itself to the right partner. Sometimes a whole section of a DNA strand gets dropped or is copied twice.

Part of a strand may come loose and then get added into another strand so that it has moved from one chromosome to another. These changes to the normal set of genes are known as **mutations.**

Causes of change

There are various causes of mutations in DNA:

- ✦ Certain types of the tiniest germs known as **viruses.**
- ✦ Some chemicals including those in certain drugs.
- ✦ Forms of energy known as radiation, such as ultraviolet, X-rays, and gamma rays.

Radiation or ***radioactivity*** *is invisible, but it can seriously damage DNA in the body's cells and cause various forms of illness.*

DNA replication copying of DNA to get two identical strands from one
mutation change in the new DNA strand that may alter the genes

Effects and problems

The effects of these changes vary. They may happen in a junk part of the DNA strand and cause no trouble. Even if they happen in a part of the strand that is a **gene,** they may not affect how the gene works. The effects also depend on if the changes happen very early in life during development as a baby or later as an adult. For example, if a DNA mistake occurs during usual body maintenance, the result may be a growth or **tumor.**

Out of control

Cells in a tumor divide too fast, out of control, because of their damaged DNA. As their numbers build up, they may become **malignant** (cancerous) and spread to other body parts. Chemicals that cause such damage are called **carcinogens.** Some of the most common are in tobacco smoke.

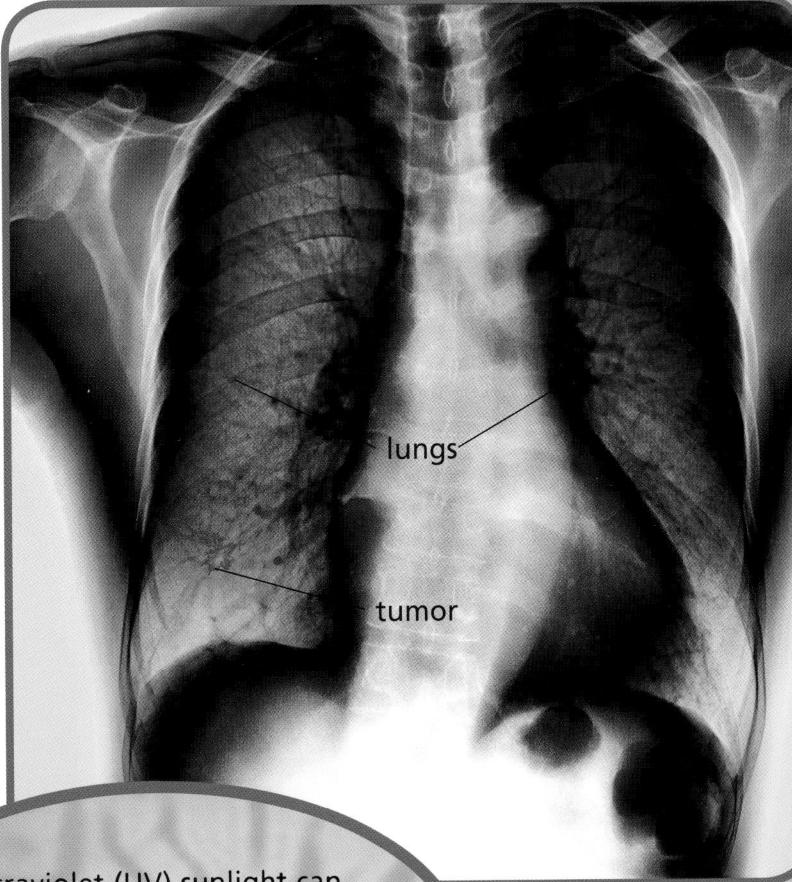

◄ Ultraviolet (UV) sunlight can damage the DNA of skin cells and cause growths, including a cancer called malignant melanoma. This picture shows up sun damage that cannot be seen in normal light.

radioactivity energy waves created when a nucleus in an atom breaks up

Passing on Genes

"What a cute new baby! She's got her mother's eyes and her father's chin." Members of the same family often look alike. We say there is a family likeness or family resemblance. Some of the similarities are clear, such as the color of skin and hair. Other similarities are less obvious, such as ear shape.

Many of these body features are passed on from parents to children to grandchildren, and so on, generation after generation. This is all due to the **genes.**

Missing out

Sometimes a grandparent has a certain body feature, the parent does not, but then the grandchild does. This usually involves the **recessive** version of a gene. We say the feature skips a **generation.**

Sometimes features like red hair skip a generation because of the way genes work.

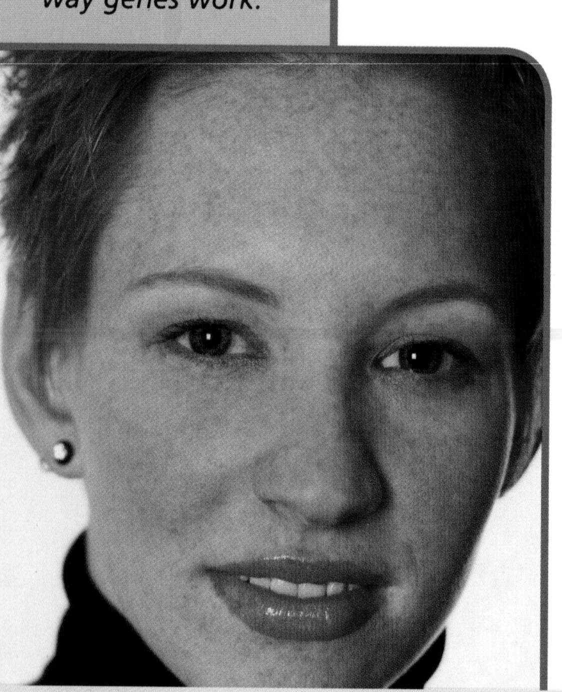

Family likeness is strongest between ➤ parents and children, since their genes are most similar. The resemblance gets less with more distant relations such as aunts, uncles, and cousins.

generation different age groups in a family, such as children, parents, and grandparents

Inheritance

Each person has a double set of genes, one from the mother and one from the father. Because of the way certain genes are dominant, some of a child's body features are from one parent, and some from the other. When children grow up to become mothers or fathers, they pass on a unique selection of genes to the next child. The passing on of genes is known as **inheritance.**

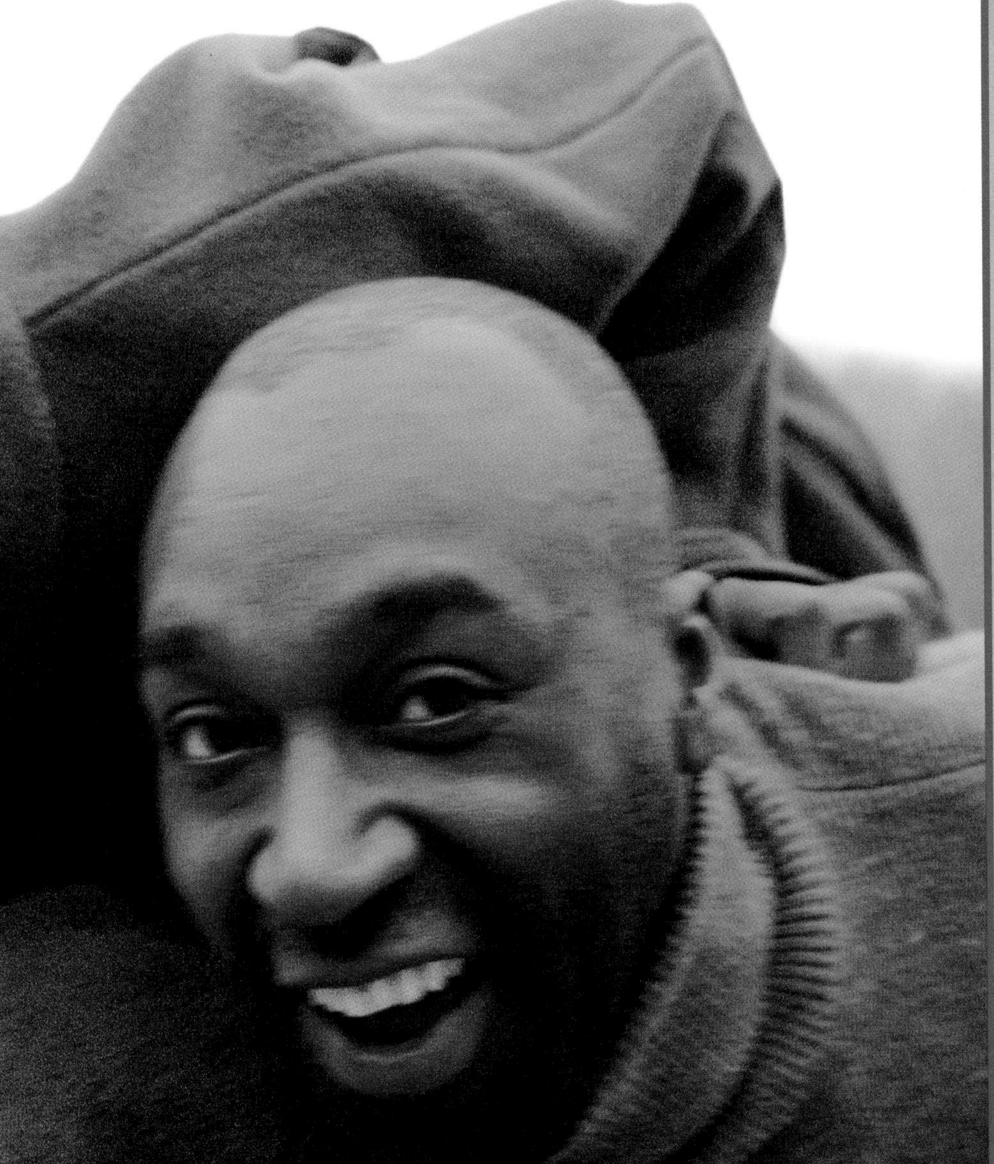

Grandparents

If you have a feature like your grandparents, but not like your parents, this is how it happened.

- The grandparent has two **recessive** versions of the gene, so the feature shows up.
- The parent inherits one recessive version, but also a dominant version from the other grandparent, so the recessive feature is overpowered.
- The grandchild inherits recessive versions from both parents and the feature returns.

inheritance passing of a characteristic from parent to child

Two ones make two

For about one day, you were a single living **cell** smaller than the dot on this i. Every human body begins as a cell like this, called the **fertilized egg.** It is made when an egg cell from the mother and a **sperm** cell from the father join together. Both the egg cell and sperm cell contain **genes.** The mother's genes in the egg come together with the father's genes in the sperm to make a new set for the baby. This is how we **inherit** genes from our parents.

Making eggs

Egg cells are made in the female body parts called **ovaries.** As with sperm cells, each egg contains only one set of genes, not the usual two.

DIFFERENT

The egg cell (below) is rounded and about 0.004 inch (0.1 millimeter) across, which is huge compared to ordinary body cells.

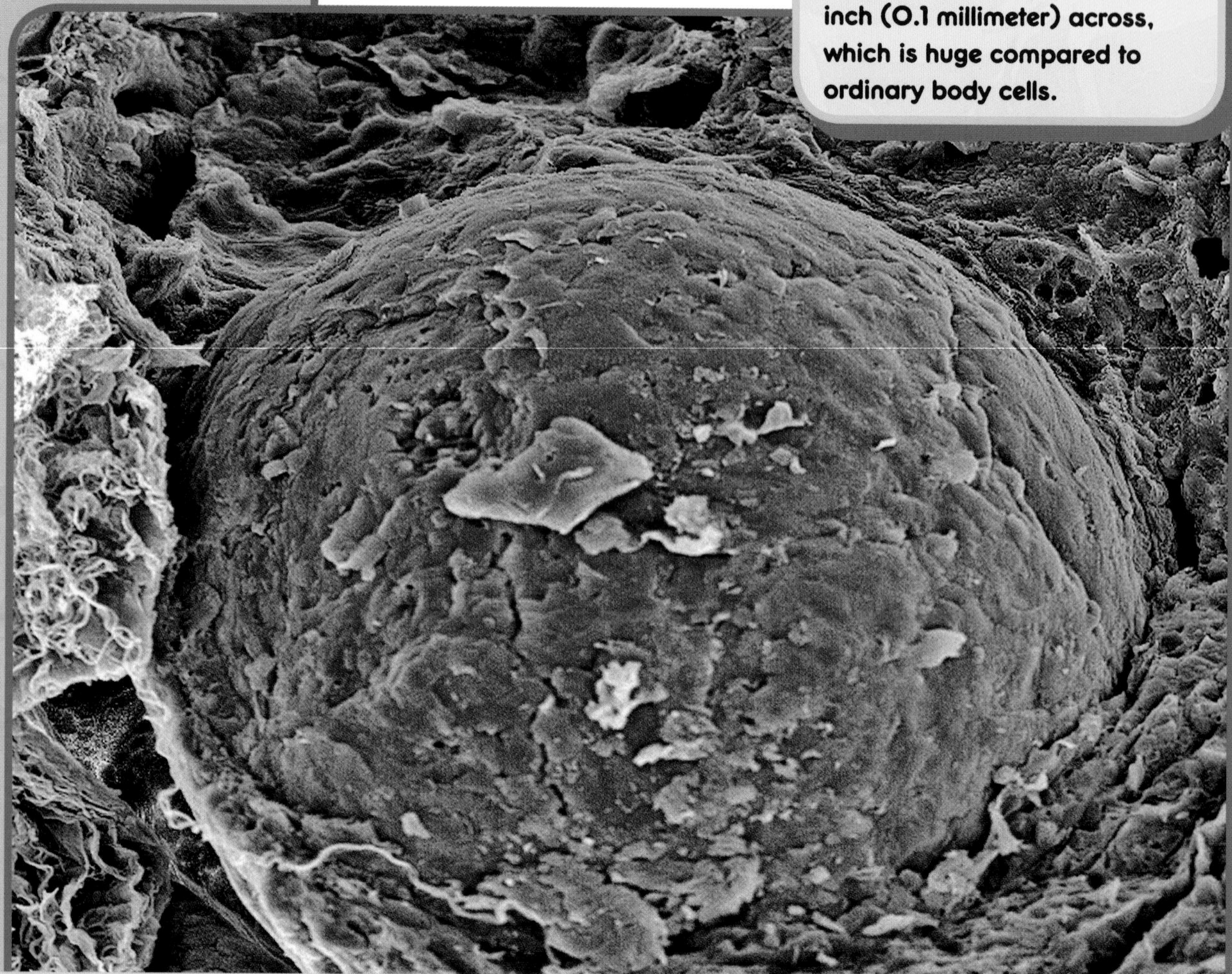

meiosis cell division that forms egg and sperm cells. Each cell gets only one set of chromosomes.

Doubling each time

But there is a catch. Both parents have a complete double-set of genes in each body cell. If the egg and sperm cells had these, then when they joined, the fertilized egg would have four sets. This does not happen because egg and sperm cells are made by a special kind of cell division called **meiosis.**

One set only

When a cell with two complete sets of genes divides by meiosis, each resulting cell receives only one of the complete sets. This happens to egg and sperm cells. When the egg and sperm join, the two single sets come together to make the usual double set in the fertilized egg. The egg can now begin normal cell division by mitosis to start forming the baby's body.

Making sperm

Sperm cells are made in the male body parts called **testes.** Each sperm contains only one set of genes, not the usual two as in other body cells.

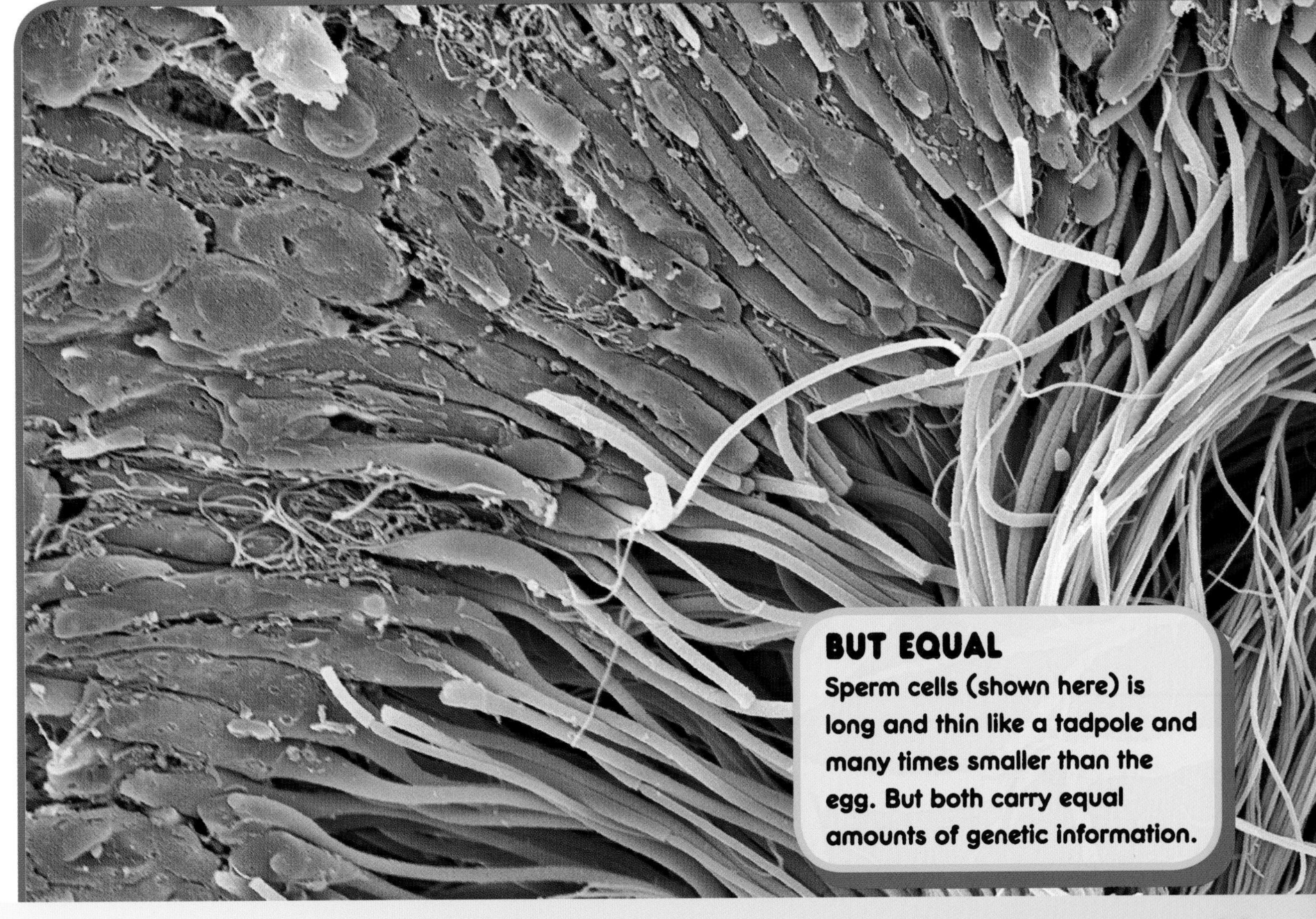

BUT EQUAL

Sperm cells (shown here) is long and thin like a tadpole and many times smaller than the egg. But both carry equal amounts of genetic information.

sperm cell cell made by the male body

Female reproductive parts

One of the first questions about you when you were born was "is it a boy or a girl?" Male and female bodies have mostly the same parts, like skin, muscles, heart, lungs, and stomach. But some important parts are not the same. These are called the reproductive parts, because they are used for **reproduction** which makes babies.

Female parts

The female reproductive parts are all inside the lower **abdomen** (unlike the male ones). They begin to develop during puberty, which usually begins at the age of 10–13 years.

Egg release

In the female reproductive parts, the egg cells are formed in two rounded **ovaries.** Every 28 days or so, one egg cell becomes bigger and ripe, and breaks out of the ovary's surface. It moves slowly along a tube called the **oviduct,** towards the **womb,** a journey that takes four or five days.

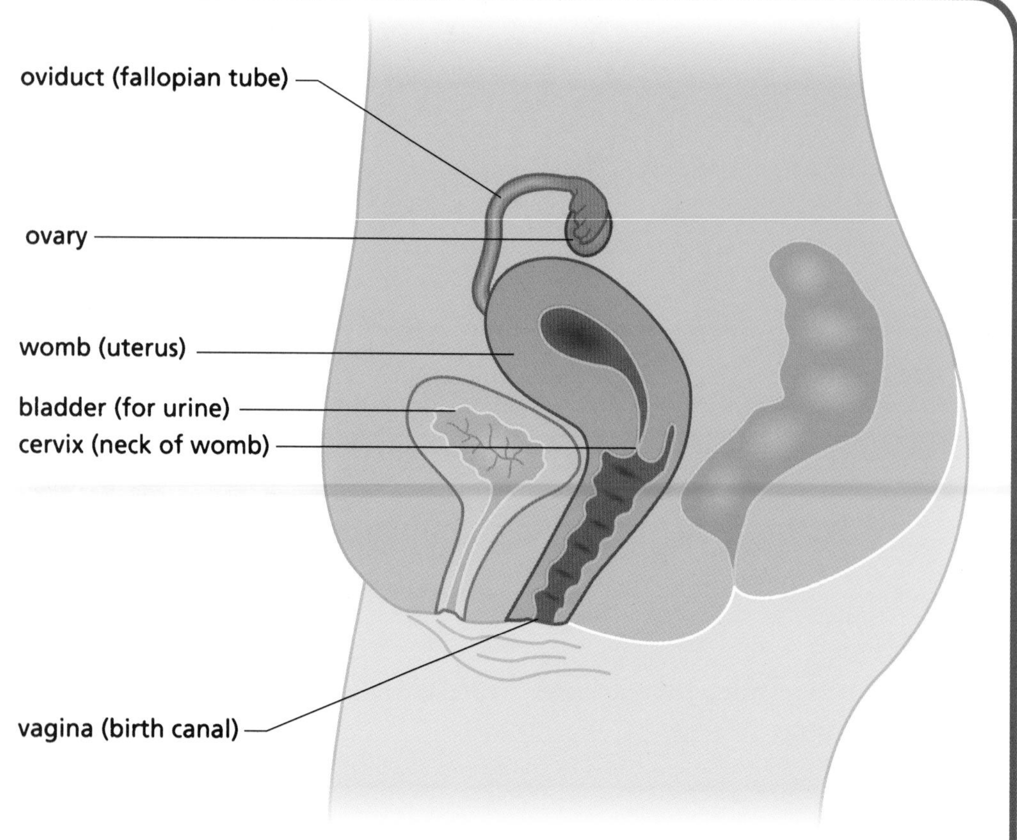

abdomen lower part of the body or torso
puberty age when sexual or reproductive parts begin to work

The female cycle

Over the seven to ten days before the ripe egg is released, the inner lining of the womb has become thick with many tiny **blood vessels.** It is making itself ready to nourish the egg if it gets fertilized.

If there is no fertilized egg, the womb lining breaks into pieces. It passes along the **vagina** (birth canal) and out of the body as bleeding called a period or **menstruation.** Then the whole process of releasing a ripe egg begins again.

This whole process is called the menstrual cycle. It is controlled by natural messenger substances in the body, mainly the **hormones,** estrogen and progesterone.

Egg cell numbers

- By the time a baby girl is born, up to half a million egg cells have already been made in her ovaries.
- This number is about 200,000 by the time of puberty, due to natural wearing out of cells.
- During the fertile years, when a woman can have babies, about 400 eggs become ripe and are released, one after the other, with each menstrual cycle.

◀ The reproductive parts of the body are the only ones that do not work during childhood. They begin to do so in **puberty.**

womb female body part where a baby develops

Male parts

The main male reproductive parts are below the lower abdomen. Every day millions of sperm are formed. If they do not leave during ejaculation, they harmlessly break apart and the leftovers are taken back into the body.

Male reproductive parts

In the male reproductive parts, sperm cells are formed in two rounded **testes,** also known as **testicles.** Unlike egg cells, which are released every 28 days, sperm cells are made all the time, thousands every second. They begin as microscopic blobs in about 800 tiny narrow tubes called **seminiferous tubules,** tightly coiled within each testis. Over several weeks the sperm cells change shape, becoming long and thin, with a rounded head and long, flexible tail.

Ready to leave

When sperm cells are fully formed, they are stored in another coiled tube next to the testis, the **epididymis.** To leave the body and join an egg cell, they pass from here along a curving tube, the **sperm duct.**

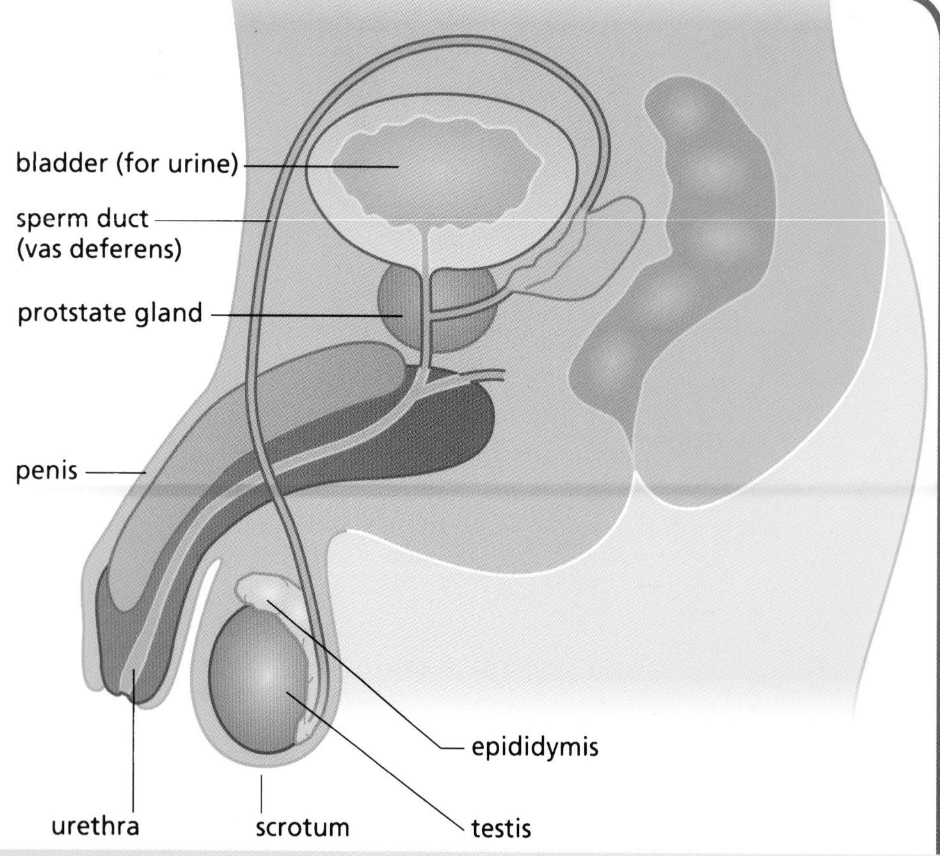

ejaculation muscle-powered action that pushes sperm through the sperm duct out of the penis

The sperm ducts from the two testes join inside a part known as the **prostate gland.** This adds fluid to the sperm, to give them energy so they can swish their tails and swim along.

The final journey

The sperm in their fluid then pass along a final tube, the **urethra.** This is inside another male part, the **penis.** The urethra carries the sperm to the outside by the muscle-powered action of **ejaculation.** The production of sperm cells is controlled by **hormones.** The main male hormone is testosterone.

Numbers of sperm cells

- ✦ No sperm cells are made in the body until the time of puberty.
- ✦ After this, millions of sperm cells are made every day.
- ✦ Around 300 million to 500 million sperm cells are released in each ejaculation.

◀ From about 10–13 years old, the bodies of girls and boys become more different, mainly as the result of the hormones made by their reproductive parts.

prostate gland part in the male body that adds fluid to sperm cells as they are released
seminiferous tubules coiled tubes in the testis where sperm cells are made

One only

After one sperm cell has joined the egg cell at fertilization, the egg develops a hard outer layer to keep away other sperm cells. Otherwise it would receive too many sets of genes and could not develop properly.

Getting together

Egg and sperm cells carry only one set of genes. For a human body to develop, it needs the normal double set in each cell. This is formed when an egg cell and **sperm** cell come together, usually in the egg tube (**oviduct**) of the mother. The egg cell has traveled from the nearby **ovary,** probably only a thumb's length away. The sperm cells have a much longer journey, almost 1.5 feet (0.5 meter).

If one of the sperm cells enters ➤ the egg cell at **conception,** a new combination of genes is formed from a selection of the mother's and father's genes.

conception egg cell and sperm cell join to form a fertilized egg

Long journey

During **ejaculation**, the sperm cells pass out of the father's body. If this happens during **sexual intercourse**, the male **penis** is inside the female **vagina**, so the sperm cells can swim into the womb, through it, and out along the two oviducts.

Millions of sperm cells die on this huge journey, and many go into the wrong oviduct where there is no egg.

Genes come together

Finally some sperm cells reach the egg cell. One of them pushes up against it, and its head end joins with the outer layer of the egg cell. The 23 **chromosomes** inside the sperm cell's head, each one a strand of **DNA**, pass to the inside of the egg cell. Here they meet the 23 DNA strands of the egg cell. The father's genes and mother's genes have come together as a new, unique double set, ready to control the development of the new baby.

Medical help

Sometimes a woman and man cannot have a baby in the usual way, by sexual intercourse. Eggs taken from the woman's body can be mixed in a dish with sperm from the man. After fertilization in the dish, the developing egg is put into the woman's womb, to grow. This type of **infertility** treatment is known as IVF, in vitro fertilization, or the test-tube baby method.

GENETIC COUNSELING

Illnesses and problems caused by faulty genes are called genetic conditions. People with a family history of a genetic condition that makes life difficult for them can receive help from an expert, a genetic counselor. The counselor advises on the risk of it being passed on to their children.

In medical research, an egg cell can have its own genetic material removed and replaced with another set.

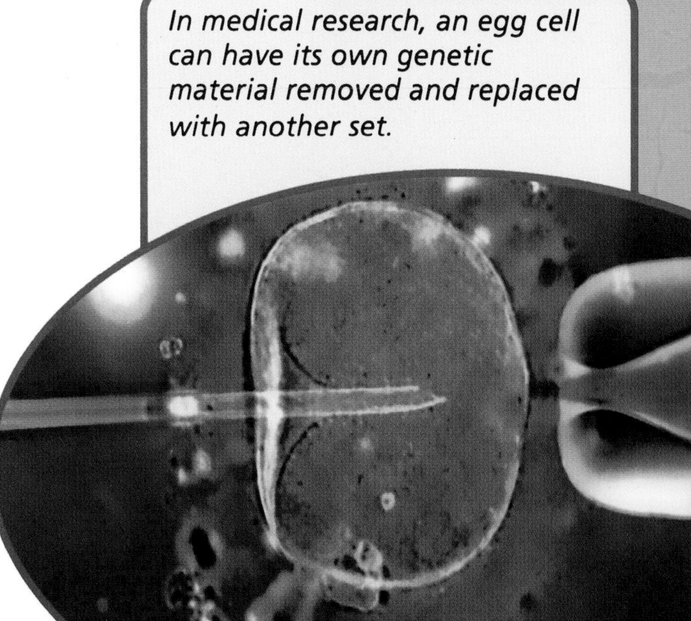

infertility a man and woman have difficulty in conceiving a baby

New Baby

Every new human body starts as a single dot-sized **cell,** the **fertilized egg,** but not for long. After a few hours it starts to divide by the normal method, copying all its **genes** first so each resulting cell has the full double set. A few hours later it happens again, and so on. After a few days there is a ball-like shape of several hundred cells. This attaches into the thick lining of the **womb,** takes in nourishment, and continues to grow.

Girl or boy?

Genes tell the new baby to develop as a girl or boy. This happens because of two **chromosomes** called sex chromosomes. They are the 23rd of the 23 pairs of chromosomes.

The other 22 pairs of chromosomes have numbers, pair 1, pair 2, and so on. The 23rd pair of sex chromsomes are named with letters, X and Y. In the cells of a man this pair is one large X chromosome and a smaller Y chromosome. In the cells of a woman they are both the same, X and X.

More than one baby

Sometimes two or more egg cells are released during the female cycle, and are fertilized by sperm cells. So two or more babies grow at the same time in the womb. Two are twins, three are triplets, and four are quadruplets. They can be all boys, all girls, or a mixture. Their genes are as similar to each other as those of any brothers and sisters.

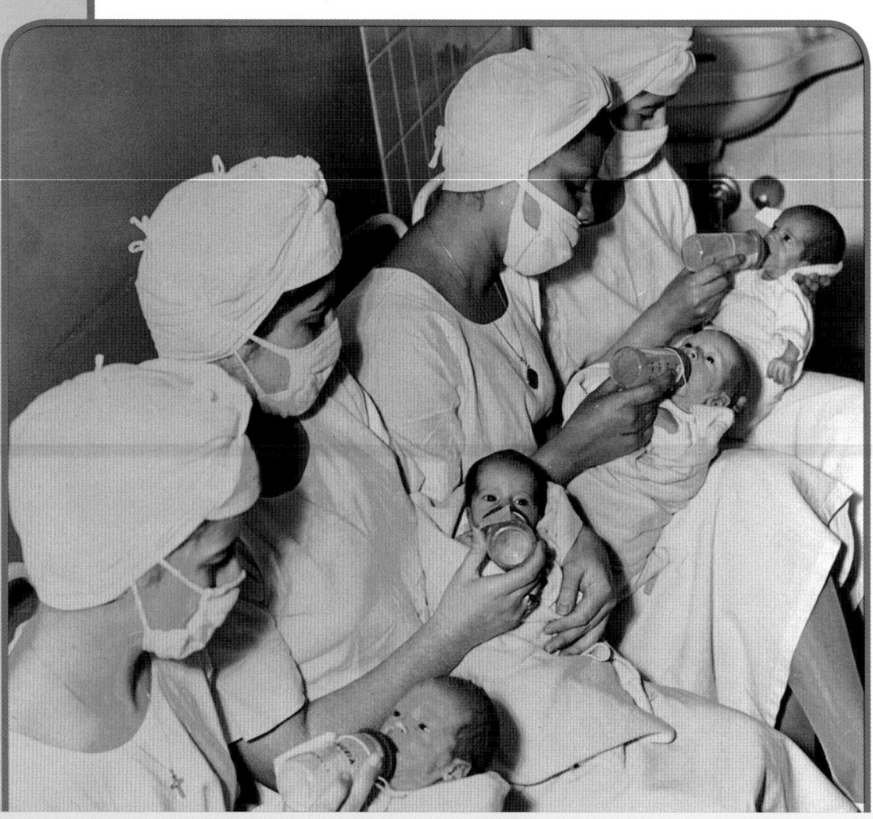

X and Y

As egg cells form in a woman, each always gets one X chromosome. When a **sperm** cell forms in a man, it can receive either an X or a Y. When an egg and sperm join, the two sex chromosomes get together. The Y chromosome contains the genes to make a male baby, and these are more **dominant** than the X genes for a female baby.

So, if an X-carrying sperm cell joins an X-containing egg cell, the result is XX, and a baby girl will develop. But if the sperm cell has a Y, the result is XY, so the developing baby will be a boy.

ARE YOU XX OR XY?

Y is more dominant than X in the sex chromosomes, so a Y chromosome from the father means the baby will be a boy.

Mother's chromosome	Father's chromosome	Baby's sex
X	X	female
X	Y	male

Identical twins

Sometimes one fertilized egg divides into two cells, then these separate and each continues to develop into a baby. The result is identical twins. They have exactly the same genes and look almost exactly alike.

Once, we all looked like this four-celled early embryo. It was made when the original fertilized egg cell divided, and each resulting cell divided again.

Life in the womb

The start of a human body is a very busy time for **genes**. The **cells** are dividing fast, moving around and becoming specialized as their various groups of genes switch on. They form body parts like the brain, heart, muscles, and skin. For the first eight weeks after **fertilization,** the developing baby is called an **embryo.** At the end of this time it is smaller than a thumb. Yet all its main body parts are formed, even its little fingers and toes, according to the **genetic** instructions.

Pregnancy

From eight weeks until birth, the developing baby is called a **fetus.** It grows a lot, and its body parts become bigger and stronger. Genetic instructions continue to work as finishing touches are added to its body, such as fingernails and toenails.

The whole time of growth in the womb is called pregnancy and lasts about nine months.

Warm and dark

The baby floats in a pool of fluid inside its mother's **womb.** It doesn't breathe air or eat food. It gets all it needs from its mother, through the **placenta.** This also forms according to genetic instructions.

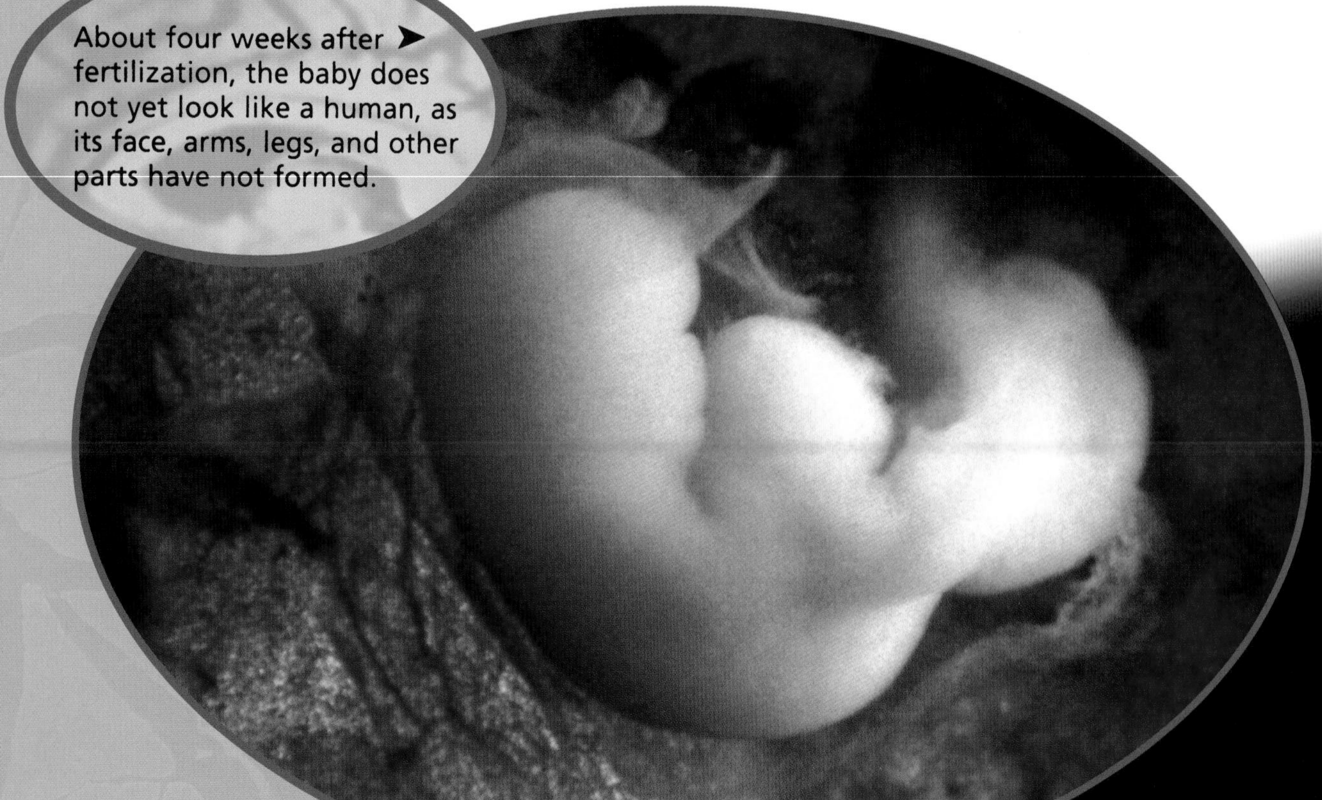

About four weeks after ➤ fertilization, the baby does not yet look like a human, as its face, arms, legs, and other parts have not formed.

placenta part in the wall of the womb that passes oxygen and nourishment from mother to baby

First check-up

During pregnancy, the mother usually has an **ultrasound scan** to see the baby inside. This gives early warning if the baby is not developing properly, perhaps because of a problem in its genes.

A gene problem could be passed on from its parents, as an **inherited** condition. Or it could be a new problem that has cropped up in the baby's own genes, as a result of a **mutation.**

About eight weeks after fertilization, the baby begins to look like a tiny human being, as it passes from the embryo to the fetus stage.

Ultrasound scan

One or two scans are usually taken between 10 and 28 weeks after the start of pregnancy. Very high-pitched sound waves beam into the womb and bounce back off the baby's body parts. These echoes are combined by computer to show a picture of the baby on a screen.

Some mothers wish to give birth in hospital, where medical help is at hand. Others prefer the familiar quiet sounds of home.

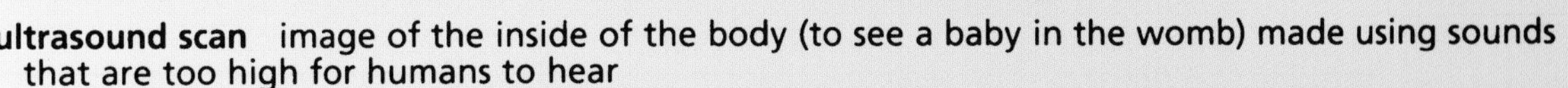

ultrasound scan image of the inside of the body (to see a baby in the womb) made using sounds that are too high for humans to hear

It's your birthday!

After nine months the baby is ready to leave the **womb** at birth. Its **genes** have guided its growth and development from a single **fertilized egg cell**, into a body made of millions of millions of cells, often weighing more than 6.6 pounds (3 kilograms). The original dot-sized egg cell has increased in size 10 billion times!

Leaving the womb

After the wet, dark, quiet, cramped warmth of the womb, the baby comes into the brighter, cooler, noisier, drier outside world. It begins to breathe for itself, usually opening up its airways by crying loudly. It also feeds for itself, usually from its mother's milk. Its life may seem to be just beginning, but its unique set of genes has already been together for months.

A lot of babies

Around the world, new sets of genes are being made every three seconds because this is how often a new baby is born.

At 4-6 months, the fetus starts to stretch, kick and suck its thumb.

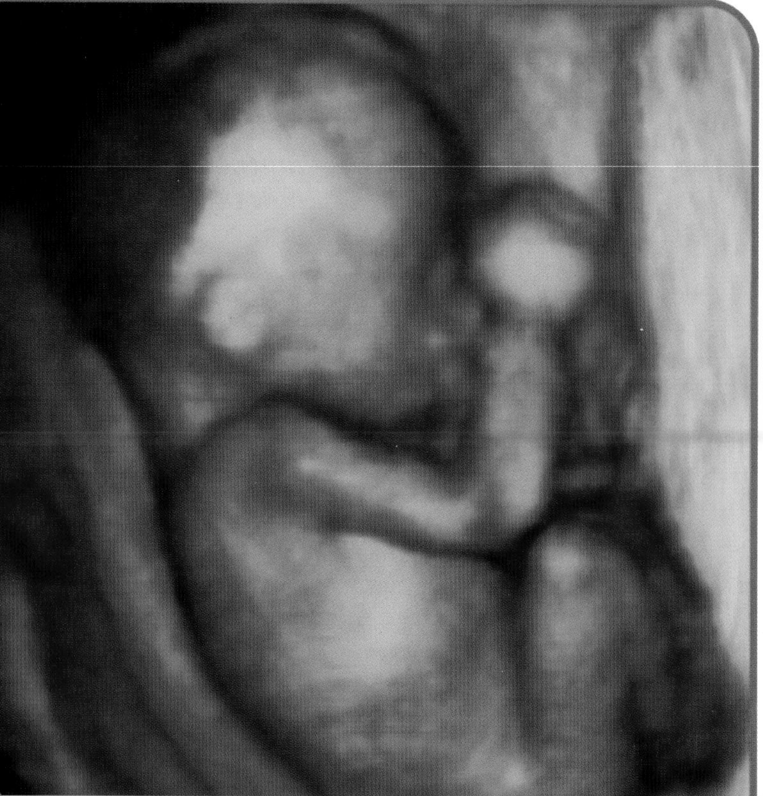

The minutes and hours ➤ after birth are very precious, as the baby and mother rest and get to know each other

Genetic problems

Rarely, birth shows that the new baby has a **genetic** problem. This might be the way its body has developed. For example, it might have one finger less or one too many, or a cleft palate which is a gap in the roof of its mouth. Usually doctors carry out operations as soon as possible to treat the problem.

Other genetic problems may not show up until later, perhaps affecting the baby's heart or the way its brain works.

Not all in the genes

As we grow up, **genes** have many effects on our lives. They shape features such as skin color, hair type, and our height as an adult. We cannot alter our genes, although medical scientists are trying to develop new treatments. This is called **gene therapy,** and it is being done to treat various **inherited** and **genetic** conditions.

Too many chromosomes

Down's syndrome is a genetic condition caused by having three copies of **chromosome** number 21 in each body cell, instead of the usual two. It has various effects on appearance and how the brain works. Yet many people with the condition (like the boy in the center here) make great personal achievements.

Different conditions

Imagine shiny new cars rolling off the production line. They all start out much the same. But after several years, they are different, depending on the care their owners take. Some of the cars might be serviced and cleaned often, still look good, and run well. Others suffer neglect, breakdowns, and accidents, and look dirty and damaged. A few are already in the scrap yard.

gene therapy treating a medical condition by altering or replacing faulty genes

Taking care

Like the cars, our bodies respond to how we take care of them. This includes the food we eat, our activities and sports, how we behave, our relationships with family and friends, the likes and dislikes we develop, how hard we try at school, and many other aspects of daily life.

Your genes have a lot of say in what you will become. But so do your surroundings and environment. And, as you get older, so do the choices you make for yourself.

Gene therapy

Medical research is trying to find ways of changing faulty genes. Gene therapy has been used to replace faulty cells with normal cells, so they will multiply and take over. Results so far are mixed, but gene therapy is a great hope for the future.

◀ Our genes have many effects, especially on the appearance of our bodies, but so do our personal choices and behavior.

Find Out More

Where to search

Search engine
A search engine looks through millions of Web site pages. It lists all the sites that match the words in the search box. It can give thousands of links, but you will find the best matches are at the top of the list, on the first page. Try **google.com**

Search directory
A search directory is like a library of Web sites that have been sorted by a person instead of a computer. You can search by keyword or subject and browse through the different sites like you look through books on a library shelf. A good example is **yahooligans.com**

Books

Brynie, Faith Hickman. *101 Questions about Reproduction.* Minneapolis, MN: Lerner Publishing, 2006

O'Donnell, Kerri. *The Reproductive System.* New York: Rosen Publishing, 2000

Parker, Steve. *Reproduction.* Chicago: Raintree, 2004

World Wide Web

If you want to find out more about genes and reproduction, you can search the Internet using keywords like these:

- "identical twins"
- sperm + egg
- double helix

You can also find your own keywords by using headings or words from this book. Use the search tips below to help you find the most useful Web sites.

Search tips

There are billions of pages on the Internet. It can be difficult to find exactly what you are looking for. These tips will help you find useful Web sites more quickly:

- Know what you want to find out about.
- Use two to six keywords in a search, putting the most important words first.
- Be precise—only use names of people, places, or things.
- If you want to find words that go together, put quote marks around them, for example, "stomach acid."
- Use the advanced section of your search engine.
- Use the + sign between keywords to link them.

Glossary

abdomen lower part of the body or torso
adenine one of the four chemical units in DNA called bases
allele version of a gene that controls how a certain body part is made or works
bases four chemicals that form the rungs of the ladder in DNA. Each rung is made of two bases.
blood vessels arteries, capillaries and veins through which blood flows
carcinogens substances that trigger cancerous growths or tumors
cell division one cell splits to make two cells
cells microscopic building blocks that make up all living things
chromosome thread of DNA that contains thousands of genes
conception egg cell and sperm cell join to form a fertilized egg
cytosine one of the four chemical units in DNA called bases
DNA deoxyribonucleic acid. Molecule that contains the genes.
DNA polymerase enzyme that enables DNA to copy itself
DNA replication copying DNA to get two identical strands from one
dominant one version of a gene is stronger than another (which is called recessive), so its genetic instructions are followed
double helix shape of the chemical DNA
ejaculation muscle-powered action that pushes sperm from the sperm duct out of the penis
embryo developing baby from fertilization to eight weeks old
epididymis coiled tube in the testis where sperm are stored
fallopian tube another name for the oviduct tube from the ovary to the womb
fertilized egg egg cell joined with a sperm cell
fetus developing baby in the womb, from eight weeks old until birth
gene therapy treating a medical condition by altering or replacing faulty genes
generation different age groups in a family, such as children, parents, and grandparents
genes instructions for how the body grows, develops, and works. Smallest unit that can pass characteristics from one person to another.
genetic to do with genes
genetic condition medical problem due to a problem in the genes
genetic fingerprint code on a strand of DNA, unique to each person
guanine one of the four chemical units in DNA called bases
hormones substances made by glands that spread around the body in the blood and affect or control the way that various parts work
human genome complete set of genes for the human body
infertility a man and woman have difficulty in conceiving a baby

inheritance passing of a characteristic from parent to child

malignant when growths or tumors spread to other body parts, as in many types of cancer

meiosis cell division that forms egg and sperm cells. Each cell only gets one set of chromosomes.

menstruation the womb lining passes out through the vagina of the body

mitosis type of cell division where each of the two new cells gets a full double set of chromosomes (two sets of all the genes)

mutation change in the new DNA strand that may alter the genes

nerves stringlike tissues that carry messages around the body as tiny pulses of electricity

nucleus control center of a cell. It contains the DNA.

ovaries two female body parts that make egg cells and hormones called estrogen and progesterone

oviduct tube from the ovary to the womb in the female body, also known as the fallopian tube

oxygen gas that makes up one-fifth of air, and which the body needs

penis male body part through which sperm are released and urine passes from the bladder

pigment substance with a particular color in paints, or in skin, hair, and the eye

placenta part in the wall of the womb that passes oxygen and nourishment from mother to baby

prostate gland part in the male body that adds fluid to sperm cells as they are released

proteins substances in the body that come from foods and are used mainly for building and growing

puberty age when sexual or reproductive parts begin to work

radioactivity energy waves created when a nucleus in an atom breaks up

recessive one version of a gene is weaker than another (which is called dominant), so its genetic instructions are not followed

red blood cells cells specialized to carry oxygen around the body

reproduction living things make more of their kind

ribosomes parts within a cell, where simple chemical substances are joined together to make proteins according to RNA instructions

RNA ribonucleic acid. It uses genetic instructions from DNA to build proteins inside cells.

seminiferous tubules coiled tubes in the testis where sperm cells are made

sexual intercourse when a woman and man get together and the man's penis is inside the woman's vagina

sperm cell cell made by the male body that joins with a female's egg cell to become a fertilized egg

sperm duct tube in the male body through which sperm cells are released from the testis to the penis

stem cells cells that can make specialized cells, such as blood or skin cells

testes two parts below the lower male body that make sperm cells and a hormone called testosterone

testicles another name for the testes

thymine one of the four chemical units in DNA called bases

tumor unnatural lump or growth, usually caused by cells multiplying too fast and out of control

ultrasound scan image of the inside of the body (to see a baby in the womb) made using sounds that are too high for humans to hear

urethra tube that carries the urine from the bladder out of the body

uterus female body part where a baby develops, also called the womb

vagina passageway from the womb to the outside, also called the birth canal

viruses tiniest germs, that can cause serious disease

womb female body part, also called the uterus, where a baby develops

Index

adenine 12
alleles 18, 19
animals 17

bases 12, 13, 23, 24
birth 40-41
blood cells 9, 20, 21
bone cells 8, 20, 21

cancers 25
carcinogens 24, 25
cells 8-9, 12
  blood cells 9, 20, 21
  bone cells 8, 20, 21
  cell division 10, 11, 20, 22, 25, 29, 36, 38
  egg cells 16, 28, 29, 30, 31, 34, 35, 36, 37, 40
  life span 20
  muscle cells 8, 9, 21
  nerve cells 8, 20
  nucleus 11, 14, 16, 20
  renewal 20
  ribosomes 14, 15
  skin cells 9, 20
  sperm cells 28, 29, 32, 33, 34, 35, 37
  stem cells 20-21
chromosomes 10-11, 12, 14, 35, 42
  copying 22
  pairs 16-17, 22
  sex chromosomes 36-37
conception 34, 35
cytosine 12

dimples 18
DNA (de-oxyribonucleic acid) 6, 7, 9, 10, 12, 14, 20
  bases 12, 13, 23, 24
  chromosomes 10-11, 12, 14, 16-17, 22, 35, 36-37, 42
  DNA polymerase 22, 23
  DNA replication (copying DNA) 22-24
  double helix 12, 13
  junk DNA 12, 25
  mutations 24-25, 39
dominant genes 18, 19, 27, 37
double helix 12, 13
Down's syndrome 42

earlobes 18-19
egg cells 28, 29, 30, 31, 34, 35, 37
  fertilized egg 16, 28, 29, 31, 34, 35, 36, 37, 40
ejaculation 32, 33, 35
embryo 38
epididymis 33
eyelashes 19
eyes 15

family likeness 5, 26, 27
feet 19
fingerprints 8, 44
  genetic fingerprint 22, 23
fetus 38, 39
Fragile X Syndrome 41

genes 4, 5, 6, 7, 9, 10, 11, 12
  alleles 18, 19
  copying 14-15, 36
  dominant genes 18, 19, 27, 37
  gene therapy 42, 43
  gene-switching 9
  recessive genes 19, 26, 27
  genetic code 12
  genetic conditions 35, 39, 41, 42
  genetic counselling 35
  genetic fingerprint 22, 23
  genetic information 12, 14, 17, 29, 38
guanine 12

hair 19
hormones 31, 33
human genome 6, 7

illnesses 25, 35, 41
infertility treatment 35
inheritance 27, 28, 39
IVF (in vitro fertilization) 35

junk DNA 12, 25

meiosis 28, 29
menstruation 30, 31
mitosis 22, 29
muscle cells 8, 9, 21
mutations 24-25, 39

nerve cells 8, 20
nucleus 11, 14, 16, 20

ovaries 28, 30, 34
oviduct 30, 34
oxygen 9

penis 33, 35
physical appearance 4, 26
pigments 14, 15
placenta 38
plants 17
pregnancy 38-39
prostate gland 32, 33
proteins 14, 15
puberty 30, 31

radiation 24, 25
recessive genes 19, 26, 27
reproduction
  birth 40-41
  conception 34, 35
  pregnancy 38-39
  sexual intercourse 35
reproductive parts
  female 30-31
  male 32-33
ribosomes 14, 15
RNA (ribonucleic acid) 14-15

seminiferous tubules 32, 33
sex chromosomes 36-37
sexual intercourse 35
skin cells 9, 20
sperm cells 28, 29, 32, 33, 34, 35, 37
stem cells 20-21

testes (testicles) 29, 32
testosterone 33
thymine 12
tumours 25
twins, triplets and quads 4, 36, 37

ultrasound scan 39
ultra-violet (UV) light 24, 25

vagina 31, 35
viruses 24

womb 30, 31, 35, 36, 38, 39, 40